"27"

How it's going
so Far...

TREVER D. OVERTON

Trever Overton

CONTENTS

This book is dedicated to Lauryn Elizabeth Overton & Chancelor Deon Overton. The two mentioned, are my children. I will not get into details of how much they mean to me and what I would do for them - However, I want the world to know that I dedicate the beginning of my journey as an author, to my children.

~ One ~

At 27 Years of age, I have acquired a sense of judgement that has become so solid, I wouldn't question it in a million years. So solid, in fact, that I've intentionally left relationships.

KNOWING that it wouldn't lead to the best interest of my well-being. So solid that I have even managed to avoid peer pressure before the opportunity even presented itself to me. I am even at the point in my life where I trust myself like no other.

I know, with certainty, that I would not bring harm to myself or do anything to jeopardize my life's work but...

Why do I feel like I am not where I intended to be? Why do I still feel as if I'm limiting myself and holding back the things that I KNOW I can achieve, but yet I still sit back and feel like I don't 'truly believe'.

Does this directly contradict my unquestionably wise judgement that I have just proclaimed over my life? Am I a hypocrite?

No. Instead, I think it is hypocrisy to even think that I can't. So, why? Why have I not taken the steps? When it comes down to it, I could make a million excuses in the world - and trust me I'm good at it - but that would be out of my character.

That would stray away from the ideal man that I would want myself to be for my children...

The truth of the matter is I have waited. waited on myself to finally come around.

However, the more I wait, the more I lose myself! The more that I think, "I will come around", the further away I get from the ground. I tell myself, "I need to do this NOW" - Before I lose who I am and have no other way of expressing these complex feelings.

This is all I have left of a pure heart. I wear my emotions on my sleeve in efforts to think it'll bring forth change. However, I still feel the same. Each phrase, each quote, word, or stanza... It is a never-ending journey into the depths of how I feel.

It's like, no matter how eloquently I'd like to construct a way for you to understand how I feel. I do not believe you could even begin to fathom the weight in which I feel.

Even if you had the empathy to understand, would you be able to bear it?

This is the beginning of a long journey and if you would like to keep up with the delicacies of my mind and heart, then please buckle up and prepare for a decade of eye-opening, mind-stretching, and unfathomable ideas to come from out of my mind and into your hands. I thank each and every one of you for purchasing my first book. It is short, but concise. I hope to inspire people around me to share their story - No matter how abstract it may seem. There will be someone who can relate in some capacity. Again, thank you all!

As a 27 year old man, I have grown in many ways. One way in particular, is the courage that I now possess - which was nonexistent at a few years ago. There was a point in time where I allowed all of the things that flowed inside of me to remain stagnant. All of my ideas to write, publish, and get involved with becoming an author myself. I did this to myself for at least 4-5 years and in that time frame, I've realized just how much time and energy I took away from MYSELF and the people around me who could benefit from my story. I cannot blame anyone for my late start - each and everyday I am working towards my goals/objectives. Without any excuse or reason to stop. I now understand my purpose is larger than myself... Welcome to a glimpse of my mind.